TM: a cosmic confi

In this series

TM: a cosmic confidence trick

Transcendental Meditation analysed

John Allan

Inter-Varsity Press

Inter-Varsity Press
38 De Montfort Street, Leicester LE1 7GP, England

First published 1980

British Library Cataloguing in Publication Data

Allan, John
   TM, a cosmic confidence trick.
   1. Transcendental meditation
   I Title
   181'.45   BF637.T68

  ISBN 0 85110 243 3

Printed in Great Britain by
Hunt Barnard Printing Ltd.,
Aylesbury, Bucks.

*Inter-Varsity Press is the publishing division of the
Universities and Colleges Christian Fellowship (formerly
the Inter-Varsity Fellowship), a student movement linking
Christian Unions in universities and colleges throughout
the British Isles, and a member movement of the
International Fellowship of Evangelical Students. For
information about local and national activities in Great
Britain write to UCCF, 38 De Montfort Street,
Leicester LE1 7GP.*

Preface

This book contains the fruits of a great deal of research, and most of it is not mine. It would be most unfair not to give credit to Pete Meadows and Lindsay Tuffin of *Buzz* magazine, for getting me involved in the first place; Caryl Williams of Deo Gloria Trust, for her ready help on all such matters; my wife Anthea, for her never-failing good humour and invaluable secretarial help; and most particularly Spiritual Counterfeits Project of Berkeley, California, from whose wealth of research I have borrowed with unashamed avarice. To them, and in particular their director Brooks Alexander, this book is admiringly dedicated.

Contents

1
Prologue

Once there was a village of farmers, set on the east bank of a wide river, which divided the village's farming land into two. It was a prosperous village, and one year there was such a surplus of food that the villagers started to build storehouses in order to conserve the extra grain. As time went by, and this continued, the villagers became so wealthy that there was no longer any need to cross the river to farm; the fields on the east side supplied all the village's needs.

After several years, no one was bothering to cross the river, and the boats had rotted away at their moorings. All the men who knew how to build boats had either died or moved on. And so it came about, after many generations, that all knowledge of the good land on the west bank was forgotten. But the village's population was growing, and after a few years of drought poverty set in. There was no longer enough food to go round.

One day, a young man from the village climbed a mountain close by, and caught sight of the fertile land across the river. He told the others, but the knowledge only increased their sorrow; the land was close at hand, but how could they get across the river to use it? Then there came to the village a very wise old man.

He told the villagers about boats, and instructed the younger men in the art of shipbuilding. Before leaving, he set up a school of boatbuilding, so that the vital knowledge would never be lost again. The villagers crossed the river, rediscovered the bountiful lost fields, and became a prosperous people once again.

And that, said Denny Gillett – the Californian meditator who told the parable[1] – is exactly what Maharishi has done for the human race.

[1] Quoted in Jack Forem, *Transcendental Meditation, Maharishi Mahesh Yogi and the Science of Creative Intellect* (London, 1974), p. 201ff.

2
Birth of a bandwagon

What Maharishi has done for the human race may or may not be valuable. But his bitterest enemy could not deny that Mahesh Prasad Warna, born in Jubblepore in 1911, has had an unaccountable impact on the Western world in the latter half of the twentieth century. Maharishi began his career as a physics student at Allahabad University, graduating at the age of 31; after which he worked in a factory for about five years, developing an interest in the Hindu Vedic scriptures on the side. But then one day he met Guru Dev.

Guru Dev (the name means 'beloved teacher') was really Swami Brahmananda Saraswati, one of the four greatest Indian spiritual leaders of the day. From his birth in 1869, he had spent most of his adult life as a solitary monk, before becoming the Shankaracharya (spiritual head) of the great monastery of Jyotir Math in the Himalayas. This was quite an honour, because the chair of Shankaracharya had been vacant for 150 years (no one had been deemed worthy to occupy it) and yet it is recorded that the monks of Jyotir Math had been trying for twenty years to persuade Guru Dev to accept the position, before he finally agreed.

Guru Dev was the decisive influence on Maharishi's life. Most people honoured him – Indian poets hailed him as a divinity, Radhakrishnan himself called him 'Vedanta Incarnate' – and Maharishi, his personal student, absolutely worshipped him. Whenever Maharishi speaks in public nowadays, a picture of his Guru is always on the dais behind him.

Saraswati seems to have given Maharishi the basic ideas of Transcendental Meditation. He died in 1953, but even on his deathbed commanded Maharishi to go to the Himalayas to evolve a 'short cut' to the knowledge of ultimate reality.

10

Maharishi obediently went into seclusion as a hermit for two years, and then became persuaded to move south and begin teaching. His band of disciples grew (though his detractors increased as well) and eventually he chose Rishikesh, at the foot of the Himalayas, as the site of his International Academy of Meditation.

As this title would suggest, right from the start he had transcontinental ambitions. He was convinced that what he had to offer the world must not be limited to India. And so two years after he began to teach (31 December, 1957), Maharishi announced his worldwide strategy. The knowledge of meditation was to spread around the globe. And the saint responsible would henceforth be known as Maharishi ('great sage') Mahesh (his family name) Yogi ('united with God'). Under this title he visited the United States in 1961; as he shrewdly commented, 'New ideas get better acceptance in technologically developed countries.'

The West's acceptance of his new ideas was a little slow in coming, but Maharishi kept trying, fulfilling thirteen world tours and visiting fifty countries within the next decade. And eventually the West succumbed. When it did, the unlikely catalyst proved to be The Beatles.

George Harrison was the first to meet Maharishi, through his spare-time study of Indian music. Because of Harrison's enthusiasm the other Beatles accompanied him to a remote part of Wales, to study meditation with Maharishi in person.

Afterwards, John Lennon told newspaper reporters, 'This is the biggest thing in our lives.' Ringo Starr announced, 'Since meeting His Holiness, I feel great.' And Paul McCartney proclaimed expansively, 'Transcendental Meditation is good for everyone.'

With publicity like that, Maharishi's influence soared. By the end of 1965 there had been only 220 meditators involved in TM; by the end of 1968 there were 12,000. Other show-business personalities became curious – Shirley Maclaine, Donovan, even the Rolling Stones joined the exclusive circle. In 1967 the Beatles visited Rishikesh; in 1968 Mia Farrow

11

followed. What they found there was a 15-acre, fifty-eight-room, air-conditioned palace worth $750,000. TM was big business.

In 1969, it became academically respectable too, when the first university course in the 'Science of Creative Intelligence' appeared at Stanford. And then, just as success seemed complete, everything started to go sour. The Beatles became disillusioned, and publicly announced that they had 'made a mistake'. Other superstars began to dissociate themselves, describing Maharishi as an 'ageing Hindu con-man'. A nineteen-city lecture tour of the States flopped miserably, and Maharishi, who had packed out Madison Square Gardens such a short while before, became untypically disheartened. Declaring, 'I know that I have failed. My mission is over', he climbed on a jet and travelled back to Rishikesh.

When in 1970 his financial affairs were under embarrassing official scrutiny, and he had to decamp hurriedly to the Italian resort of Fiuggi Fonte, most people believed TM was disintegrating. Had this been the case, Maharishi would have been no more than a footnote in the history of curious twentieth-century Western fads. But then he bounced back.

In 1972, *Time* magazine remarked with surprise that 'the guru has generated what may well be the fastest-growing cult in the West'. By October 1972, 10,000 new meditators were being enrolled each month. In Great Britain the monthly figure (500 converts a month) compared remarkably with the Established Church's rate of adult baptisms (660 monthly): the new cult was doing nearly as well!

The year before had seen the foundation of Maharishi International University, and the first International Symposium on the Science of Creative Intelligence at the University of Massachusetts. In 1973 followed a successful World Conference of Mayors in Switzerland. Meditation began to permeate every level of society: it was made available to the US Army; adopted as an official course by over

25 universities; and examined by various State Administrations for its potential in combating drug addiction. The State of Illinois went so far as to pass a resolution 'that all educational institutions, especially under State of Illinois jurisdiction, be strongly encouraged to study the feasibility of courses in TM and SCI on their campuses and in their faculties'. The resolution also urged the US Department of Mental Health 'to study the benefits of TM' and, in so far as 'practical and medically wise, to incorporate the course of TM in the Drug Abuse programme'.[1]

Now TM has spawned the Students' International Meditation Society (aimed at college campuses), the American Foundation for SCI (reaching businessmen and leaders of industry), the Spiritual Regeneration Movement (appealing to religious leaders), and the International Meditation Society (for the general public). And growth means money.

The World Plan Executive Council is reputed to gross $1.5 million per month. In 1972 the US Department of Health, Education and Welfare lent a helping hand by deciding to invest $21,540 in training 130 public high school teachers in TM. Ever since, Transcendental Meditation has been taught in high schools right across America.

Apart from the inclusion of SCI as a course at prestigious universities (Yale and Harvard among them) Maharishi's own university has established two campuses in the USA, offering a four-year course for bachelor degrees. TM television stations are opening in America; and when in 1974 the Nepalese government appealed to Maharishi to educate Nepal in TM, the guru's gospel was spreading within a month via TV and closed-circuit video. It was the first TV broadcasting ever in Nepal's history.

Famous names have never been far from the TM movement. For his 1972 International Symposium, Maharishi managed to secure the services of Marshall Macluhan, Nobel prizewinner Donald Glaser, and Apollo 9 astronaut 'Rusty' Schweikart. Official support for TM has come from such

[1] Quoted in Kroll, p. 24.

figures as Adlai Stevenson, the Senators for California and Alaska, the Governor of Vermont, the City Council of Los Angeles, the State Legislature of Connecticut. Before his retirement, Major-General Franklin Davis, commandant of the US Army War College, advocated the teaching of TM to the army. 'The army should pick up the tab,' he insisted, 'and provide the instruction.' His successor in office was Brigadier-General Robert Gard – and he had become a meditator in 1972.

Meanwhile, in Britain and Europe, TM has grown less spectacularly, but steadily nonetheless. At the time of writing, 75,000 Britons have been initiated, and a thousand more join every month. The movement is claiming adherents among MPs, diplomats, priests, nuns and clergymen. Meditation is being taught to school pupils in at least four areas (including, in one case, primary school children); at the exclusive Millfield School, a TM exercise with certain pupils was defended by the school chaplain as 'a very good research work to undertake'.[2] Meanwhile, big business has shown interest; several major companies – notably Unilever – are reported to be working with the TM movement on pilot projects.

Maharishi has achieved an incredible come-back. And the key to the movement's fortunes, without any doubt, is the unlikely figure of its leader. He is not a charismatic personality in the usual sense, though: even his admirer Dr Anthony Campbell admits, 'Maharishi is at first sight a disappointment. I do not know quite what I expected a great spiritual teacher to be like, but certainly I did not expect this tiny figure, constantly bubbling over with laughter. He was disconcerting; he made one think of a blob of mercury, bright and mobile, unpredictable, impossible to seize. The only thing I was sure of was that he was totally unlike anyone I had ever met.'[3]

Nonetheless, there are probably three reasons why this

[2] *Buzz*, October 1977, 'Britain and the Guru', p. 4.
[3] Quoted in Kroll, p. 27.

14

particular Indian guru should have done so amazingly well. First, he rings true. Unlike the leaders of several other mystical Hindu groups, he appears to be thoroughly convinced of the value of what he is doing. Personally an abstemious man, by all accounts, he works hard and takes little time off to sleep. Not many of his detractors have found a great deal to criticize in the Maharishi's private life.

The second reason for his success must be that he has always encouraged scientific investigation of TM. Many Hindu cults have shied away from examination by the probing methods of Western science, but not the Maharishi. Physics graduate as well as Hindu monk, he has always seen TM as the 'missing link' between science and religious experience, and so welcomes detailed research into his technique. This has given him a scientific prestige and an appearance of honest openness which are useful assets in a Western society where people trust the results of 'science' yet long for something more cosmically satisfying than mere science can provide.

And, finally, Maharishi has developed a very clear idea of where he wants to go. His 'World Plan' is staggering in its scope, but imaginatively detailed too. Basing his thinking on a world population of 3,600 million, he has set himself the goal of providing one teacher of TM for every thousand people on earth. Phase One consists of opening 3,600 teacher-training centres, each of which will educate 1,000 teachers. There will also be thirty-six administration centres running 100 training centres each.

The sheer confidence and vision which can plan a campaign to win the world, and do it in such detail, can hardly fail to appeal to the idealism of a lot of young people. Maharishi not only claims that his teaching fulfils economics, the humanities, political science, the natural sciences, sociology, psychology, religion, philosophy, world peace and law; he has also planned exactly how he is going to affect those diverse realms. His World Plan Objectives are worth quoting:

15

1. To develop the full potential of the individual.
2. To enhance governmental achievements.
3. To realize the highest ideal of education.
4. To solve the problems of crime, drug abuse, and all behaviour that brings unhappiness to the family of men.
5. To maximize the intelligent use of the environment.
6. To bring fulfilment to the economic aspirations of individuals and society.
7. To achieve the spiritual goals of mankind in this generation.

Vague, perhaps, in places, but incredibly varied: any spiritual group which can so systematically and energetically plan the world's future history, with such brio and self-possession, is liable to make the world sit up and take notice.

3
How to become a normal human being

How is Maharishi going to bring about the World Plan? What exactly does he teach?

When the *Los Angeles Times* put this question to leaders of the TM movement, they 'conceded that the metaphysical base (the science of creative intellect) behind TM is a revival of ancient Brahmanism and Hinduism'.[1] This was a more open and honest admission than most TM leaders will make – as we shall see – but essentially it is the truth. Maharishi is a Hindu yogi of the *bhakti* variety. He believes that God is basically an impersonal essence, present in everything, rather than the personal God of Christian revelation. This impersonal God is called 'Brahman', and the most

[1] *Los Angeles Times*, 12 May, 1974, Part 1, p. 20.

important thing in life is to open oneself to the reality of Brahman; to become conscious of the Infinite. This world is just *maya* (illusion) and too deep an interest in the affairs of this life is harmful. By opening oneself up to Brahman, eventually one loses one's sense of individuality and becomes simply united with God.

This prompts the question: how does one open oneself up to Brahman? Hinduism has all sorts of answers, and comfortably embraces many routes to God. There are basically nine different kinds of *yoga* (the word means 'spiritual discipline') by which men can come into contact with God, and *bhakti yoga* (Maharishi's kind) is the discipline of devotion. Closeness to God is achieved by devotion to God, which can be expressed in special ways. (Another *bhakti* group, for example, is the Hare Krishna movement, in which the accepted form of devotion is chanting for hours each day.)

Maharishi's technique for showing devotion is meditation, which (he says) transcends ordinary consciousness and lifts our awareness on to a higher plane. (Hence the name 'Transcendental Meditation'.) There are, according to Maharishi, eight states of consciousness, only three of which are normally recognized in the West: wakefulness, dreaming sleep, and dreamless sleep. Through meditation it is possible to experience five more distinct states of awareness.

The first level a new meditator will reach is 'transcendental consciousness'. This is described as a state of 'restful wakefulness', and a novice will be able to achieve it only in short, concentrated periods every day.

But after meditating for a while a person should find that the state of restfulness can be maintained all day, no matter how hectic the activity in which he is engaged. At this point he has reached the level of 'cosmic consciousness' ('CC' in meditator slang), and is able to balance restfulness naturally against the life of activity. Anything less than this level of consciousness, says Maharishi, is subnormal living.

But those who wish can advance yet further. The next level is 'God consciousness' (sometimes called 'refined CC'): surrender to God's almighty will as the infinite Brahman becomes the object of one's worship. After living in this level for a while, the devotee finds his perception changing: it seems that God is no longer 'out there' as something to be worshipped, but has somehow merged with the meditator, so that he looks out on the world with God's eyes. This level is 'unity consciousness', or 'union with God'. Finally, there is an eighth level, about which much is hinted, little affirmed: 'Brahman consciousness'; and what precisely this means, Maharishi has yet to tell the waiting world.

Now, obviously, stages six, seven and eight are un-ashamedly Hindu in their interpretation of experience. But there is no need for a meditator to continue thus far unless he chooses. Maharishi claims that if one stops at level five ('CC'), the whole thing is just a neutral technique, with no sectarian religious associations. But is this the truth? Was the young Christian right, who said, 'I don't see any conflict between TM and my Christian faith. I do it every day during my quiet time'?[2] Or was he being taken for a metaphysical ride – being sold a cosmic confidence trick – by an 'ageing Hindu con-man'?

4
Beginners start here

Transcendental Meditation is surprisingly easy to learn – a fact which has probably helped to swell its popularity. Within a week the average person can be meditating quite successfully. Learning will cost him an average week's wage (or a fixed sum, in the case of students and pensioners), and

[2] Quoted in Means, p. 131.

he will be instructed personally by an approved, trained instructor.

Most people become involved in TM through attending one of the movement's free public lectures. Here the attractions of TM are expounded, with a heavy stress on the 'scientifically proven' benefits of meditation. The audience is encouraged to attend a second lecture, for a fuller explanation – and for those who do so, this is where the crunch comes. After the lecture, they are invited to commit themselves. They must agree to the fee, write down their reasons for wishing to meditate, and promise to abstain from taking drugs for at least fifteen days before starting their course of instruction.

Each new recruit is then allocated to a teacher, and told that he will be instructed over a period of four days. The first session, lasting for an hour or maybe ninety minutes, will be the important one: the technique will be explained then. The other sessions will be check-ups on how well the new meditator is doing. Before starting, however, there is the *puja* to go through.

The *puja* is an initiation ceremony, carried out by the teacher on the pupil's behalf. Meditators are always very careful to explain that although it is a ritual ceremony, no involvement or belief is necessary on the part of the pupil. All he must do is bring his teachers certain traditional gifts: flowers, fruit, his fee, and a white handkerchief. The teacher then dedicates these gifts in a simple Sanskrit ritual before teaching begins.

The names of Hindu gods are involved, but (says the movement) the ceremony is not so much a worship service as an innocuous expression of thanksgiving for the great tradition of teachers who have handed down the great secret of meditation from one generation to another throughout the centuries .We shall investigate the truth of this claim later.

From this point onwards, tuition methods are reputed to vary, but the effect is the same. The new recruit is given a *mantra*, a simple sound such as 'Eng', 'Ienga' or 'Sham', and

19

taught to repeat this word silently until it starts to pull him down into the 'emptiness' of his inner being. According to TM theory, this silent repetition is actually causing psychic vibrations which affect the meditator's mental and physiological functioning.

The new meditator is taught to keep his *mantra* to himself – never to reveal it, not even to his wife. He is not told what it means (some teachers even claim that it is meaningless), because (says the TM movement) to understand the meaning of the *mantra* would cause distraction from its purpose. Better to let a meaningless sound function as a simple catalyst, than to use a household word with lots of clogging, irrelevant associations of meaning.

What is it like to meditate? One meditator described his first experiences like this: 'You don't know you're there, but you know you've been.' Meditation is an experience of putting one's mind 'in neutral'; of minimizing the conscious activity of the brain, and slowly becoming aware of one's inner self. The TM technique is not really something completely new to the West. It is in essence the same kind of technique as that used by some medieval Christian mystics. Una Kroll quotes this illuminating passage from the English mystical work *The Cloud of Unknowing*:

Take a short word, preferably of one syllable . . . the shorter the word the better, being more like the meaning of the Spirit: a word like 'God' or 'love'. Choose one which you like, or perhaps some other, so long as it is of one syllable. And fix this word fast to your heart, so that it is always there come what may. It will be your shield and spear in peace and war alike . . . With this word you will suppress all thought under the cloud of forgetting.[1]

Similar passages can be found in Meister Eckhart or Mother Julian of Norwich. And something not unlike TM seems to lie behind the mysticism of St John of the Cross:

[1] Quoted in Kroll, p. 108.

20

The farther that I climbed the height
The less I seemed to understand
The cloud so tenebrous and grand
That there illuminates the night.
For he who understands that sight
Remains for aye, though knowing nought,
Transcending knowledge with his thought ...

If you would ask, what is its essence –
This summit of all sense and knowing:
It comes from the Divinest Presence –
The sudden sense of Him outflowing,
In His great clemency bestowing
The gift that leaves men knowing nought,
Yet passing knowledge with their thought.[2]

On a much less exalted level, the same technique has been exploited by the women's magazine *She* is a bid to help slimmers. *She*'s 'Meditation Diet' involves the following instructions:

5. When you're totally relaxed (or as free of tension as possible), watch and experience your own breathing. Notice how you inhale and exhale. Now breathe in through your nose and, as you breathe out, repeat the word 'slim' silently to yourself.
6. Keep repeating the word silently. Don't worry if you get caught off-guard and start thinking about your income tax. Just come back to the word. Let it float in and out of your mind. You'll find that your thoughts float lazily past you, completely desensitized and unable to evoke a ripple of tension from you – even thoughts about income tax!
7. After ten or fifteen minutes – even twenty, if you can spare the time – take a deep breath and slowly come out of the depths of relaxation.[3]

[2]*Poems of St John of the Cross* (Harmondsworth, 1960).
[3] *She*, April 1978, p. 90. Article by Sal Voak based on R. M. Tyson and J. R. Walker, *The Meditation Diet* (New York, 1977).

A fascinating idea; but we must return to TM. After being taught to meditate, the new recruit is sent away with instructions to try it again the same day for a period of twenty minutes, and to return within twenty-four hours for another session. In the second session (and those following), he describes his meditating experiences to the teacher, and is helped to improve his performance, encouraged, corrected, given additional suggestions. Then after four days he will probably be confident enough to go away and continue meditation of his own, for twenty minutes twice a day, without any further instruction. Soon, he is promised, the benefits will start.

He can expect increased energy, heightened creativity, reduced stress levels, and lower blood pressure. All for a week's wages.

5
Misleading evidence

Ever since 1971, when Wallace and Benson of the Harvard Medical Unit completed a pioneering research project on TM and published their results in the *American Journal of Physiology*, Maharishi's associates have been claiming loudly that the benefits of TM are scientifically demonstrable. To a civilization conditioned to accept the authority of science, this claim is a pretty striking one. And the indefatigable trumpeting of scientific evidence by the World Plan Executive Council has left the general public with the impression that TM's results are assured, reliable and beneficial. In fact, there is room for grave doubt.

But, at first sight the evidence seems unassailable. What Wallace and Benson noticed (and some of their tests were confirmed independently by British neurophysiologist Peter

Fenwick) was that eight distinct changes took place in a group of thirty-six volunteers as a result of meditation. The changes were these:

1. A mean decrease in respiration rate.
2. A lowering of the metabolic rate (which means that all life processes have been successfully slowed down, and the body has entered a state of deep relaxation).
3. A reduction in oxygen consumption.
4. A 25% reduction in cardiac output.
5. A decrease in the arterial concentration of sodium lactate (and since an increased concentration is caused by grave anxiety, this result presumably means that existing tensions are being resolved).
6. Specific EEG changes (*i.e.* in the wave-patterns in the brain).
7. An increase in skin galvanic response (another indication of decreasing anxiety).
8. Faster reaction time.[1]

Of these results, the most interesting is 6. What the EEG showed was the sporadic co-existence of two types of waves – alpha and theta – in the brain. Very simply, this means that the wave patterns normally found in alert, wide awake people were happening *at the same time as* the wave patterns normally found in sleep! Thus meditators were both 'asleep' and 'awake' at the same time! This phenomenon is not completely unknown: it has been traced in users of Zen and other relaxation yoga techniques. But only very experienced Zen masters (of twenty years' experience or more) produce theta waves, whereas TM meditators of only six months' standing could do it!

Dr Bernard Glueck and his team took this study one step further when they monitored the brains of TM initiates during the actual *puja* (initiation ceremony). At the end of the ceremony, the novice is taught to repeat his newly bestowed

[1]*American Journal of Physiology*, vol. 221 no. 3 (Sept. 1971), pp. 795–8.

mantra over and over again, more and more softly, until eventually he is no longer saying it aloud. R. D. Scott, a member of Glueck's team, records, 'At the moment during initiation when the *mantra* repetition became silent, there was a dramatic development of an unusual synchrony in the brainwave activity.'[2] Right at the moment when the secret of TM was learnt, measurable changes were taking place!

Other research has identified psychological changes through meditation (increased perceptual ability, superior perceptual motor performance, increased learning ability, reduced nervousness, aggression, depression, irritability, tension and self-doubt) and specific effects upon drug users. Wallace and Benson themselves went on to study 1,862 meditators who had previously used drugs. After twenty-one months, over 95% had stopped, and it seemed that, the harder the drug used, the more striking was the rate of success.

The case seems unanswerable. Whatever the religious trappings of the movement, TM appears to do its adherents good. Has Maharishi proved his point?

No, says Nobel prizewinner Melvin Calvin. 'Maharishi's principal business is collecting money from new acolytes. He doesn't know anything about science.'[3] No, says Harvey Brooks, Engineering Dean at Harvard: TM is surrounded by a lot of mystical nonsense, and 'all the scientists I know who have had some contact with SCI hold about the same view.'[4] No, says British researcher Peter Fenwick, in a letter to *The Times:* 'All these studies need to be looked on with reservations. Few include adequate control groups and none that I am aware of have yet used a blind control procedure where neither subject nor observer is aware of the treatment given or the aims of the experiment. Until this sort of study

[2] Scott, p. 74.

[3] *Right On*, November 1975, p. 9.

[4] *Ibid.*, p. 9.

is carried out in meditating groups it is almost impossible to draw conclusions.'[5]

In fact, some research has now applied stricter controls of this type – and the results, as we shall see in a moment, have been markedly unfavourable for TM.

It has been claimed that Maharishi devised TM 'in a way which makes it fully accessible to modern scientific techniques of investigation'.[6] This is just not so. Lots of information remains inaccessible. Scientists are not told the basis on which *mantras* are selected for different individuals; they have never been given any indication of just how the movement distinguishes one state of consciousness from another, or what the physiological and neurological characteristics of the state of 'enlightenment' are supposed to be. Most interestingly, the man whose brain could theoretically reveal the most information about the credibility of TM claims – Maharishi himself – has never made himself available for scientific tests. The data for conclusive testing just is not there.

TM claims of a 'fourth major state of consciousness', induced by meditation, have been investigated by Dr Robert Pagano and other researchers in Seattle. They conclude that there is no such state and that different meditators experience meditation in different ways: 'Meditation is an activity that gives rise to quite different states both from day to day and from meditator to meditator.'[7]

Another factor which tends to put question marks against earlier research is that no – one has ever counted how many people are initiated and then stop meditating. The movement's grandiose figures owe a lot to the fact that everyone who has undergone the *puja* is counted in. But in fact, the

[5] *The Times*, 17 May 1974.

[6] K. Wallace (President of Maharishi International University) in a monograph 'The Neurophysiology of Enlightenment' quoted by John White, 'The Scientific Case Against TM', *National Exchange*, January 1977.

[7] *Science*, 23 January 1976.

drop-out rate is probably very high. Dr Benson, for example, now admits that his drug abuse study was inadequate, because it failed to take into account, first, people who stopped meditating and went back to drugs, and second, people who were predisposed to give up drugs anyway. (Since one of the prerequisites for receiving instruction is that one should give up drugs for at least 15 days beforehand, it seems obvious that no hopeless addict is ever going to benefit from TM.)

Benson now believes that the same kind of meditation – without a *mantra* – could be self-taught from only one page of instructions. This may be an exaggeration, but there are certainly studies to suggest that the benefits of TM do not actually come from TM itself. Dr Jonathan Smith carried out two exercises to test TM: in the first, he had 49 people initiated by a local TM centre while fifty-one others were taught a daily exercise similar to TM except that it involved 'simply sitting with eyes closed, rather than sitting with eyes closed and meditating'.[8] In the second test, his subjects were taught a sort of anti-meditation technique, which entailed sitting with the eyes closed, thinking as many positive thoughts as possible. Smith found that TM had no more success in curing anxiety than either of his own two home-made methods.

Dr Leon Otis of Stanford Research Institute believes that early favourable results of early TM experiments were due to predisposition on the part of adherents. His research into this point indicated that TM produces its effects upon people who are expecting something to happen to them, and works best with certain personality types: it does not alter basic personality characteristics.

Otis suggests that TM is a form of 'desensitization' (a word used by psychologists to describe a state of allowing repressed problems and feelings to come into one's awareness). He warns, 'It would seem that those with insufficient controls to prevent the release of massive uncontrollable

[8] Scott, p. 207.

anxiety represent a potentially high-risk population for training in TM . . . without supervision.'[9]

Rory Giles seems to have been a case of this. He became involved with TM while working on the London Stock Exchange, and meditated happily for two years until everything went wrong.

'I was sitting in my office one day when I was suddenly gripped by the most terrible fear – it was absolute panic stations! I thought I was dying. I can't overemphasize this feeling that gripped me. I wouldn't wish it on my worst enemy.'

A succession of doctors did little good. 'I was a complete wreck. When I did try to go to the office, within ten minutes of sitting down, my suit would be soaking wet with sweat – straight fear.

'The doctors blamed the meditation – it had separated me from my real self.'[10]

But the most damaging research findings so far (until now simply ignored by the movement) have been those of Dr Colin Martindale. In a *Psychology Today* article he reported, 'People who practise TM regularly have few spontaneous fluctuations in their skin conductance; creative people have many.' Consequently, TM 'may have the side-effect of decreasing our ability to think creatively'. Instead of mind-control techniques leading to increased creative powers, he believes, 'mind control and creativity . . . may be inversely related'.[11]

Scientific findings simply do not bear out Maharishi's assertion that TM is a unique method, a meditation technique without equals. There is no research data to support any idea of the kind; but an increasing amount which points

[9] J. White, *Everything you want to know about TM* (New York, 1976), p. 55.

[10] 'Britain and the Guru', *Buzz*, October 1977, p. 7.

[11] C. Martindale, 'What makes creative people different?', *Psychology Today*, July 1975.

to real, unexplored dangers which the movement is just not interested in investigating.

Yet TM goes on claiming the support of scientists of all kinds. (Not always with their approval: Melvin Calvin has stated that the use of his name in Maharishi's catalogue comes 'perilously close to false advertising', while Mayo Melvin has dissociated himself completely, remarking with dry understatement, 'Maharishi is flexible in what he considers the truth.' [12] However, until Maharishi is prepared to consider properly controlled tests, performed on the basis of more explicit information from himself about the nature of different states of consciousness, with due regard to the unpleasant as well as the pleasant findings – until then, the kindest thing that can be said about Transcendental Meditation's scientific qualifications is 'Not proven'! And the evidence against continues, threateningly, to mount.

6
Deceitful claims

MODERATOR: It's not a religion?
MAHARISHI: No, it's not a religion?
MODERATOR: It has nothing to do with religion?
MAHARISHI: No, it has nothing to do with religion. Only, it enriches life; it makes life better, whether you are a physicist or a chemist, or an astrologer or a religious man ... [1]

There is nothing TM sympathizers insist upon more stubbornly than that TM is simply a neutral technique, an objective scientific device for relieving stress and achieving relaxa-

[12] *Science*, 28 March 1975, p. 1179.
[1] *Penetrating*, p. 11.

tion. Perhaps it did emerge from Indian philosophy: so what? Science emerged from mediaeval alchemy, but we do not think of today's atomic physicist as a charlatan gold-hunter . . . 'TM is a wholly practical technique,' declares Anthony Campbell, 'which does not require any prior acceptance of dogma or concepts from those who want to try it.'[2]

Prior acceptance – yes, indeed. But what happens *afterwards* to the person who becomes entangled with TM? Does he simply operate a handy little method, while remaining basically the same person, or does he drift further and further into the conditioning grip of an Eastern mindset? Maharishi himself, in his published writings (which differ remarkably from his public statements!), appears to have no doubt. 'Meditation is a process which provides increasing charm at every step on the way to the Transcendent. The experience of this charm causes faith to grow . . . [Meditation] brings faith to the faithless and dispels the doubts in the mind of the sceptic.'[3]

Even more bluntly, he states elsewhere, 'Transcendental Meditation is a path to God.'[4] Comparing this statement with the tape transcript excerpt above, it is difficult not to accuse Maharishi of sharp practice. TM *is* religious. It is a shop window for Hinduism. And teachers of meditation are told explicitly in *The Holy Tradition* (a most important secret document given to all graduating teachers) that TM can be considered a sect:

> It may be that someone, seeing us make offerings before a picture, might argue and label us a sect, and thereby try to overshadow the universality of the Spiritual Regeneration Movement . . . We accept their challenge and say: 'Yes, we hold ourselves in pride for clinging fast to the trunk which is the source of supplying nourishment to

[2] Anthony Campbell, *The Mechanics of Enlightenment* (London, 1975), p. 10.
[3] *BG*, pp. 317–319.   [4] *Meditations*, p. 59.

every branch, and if for this purpose we are labelled as a sect or an "ism" we hail that universal sect, we hail that universal "ism".'[5]

Why then does TM deny so strenuously its religious involvement? Charles Lutes betrayed the real motive unexpectedly in an unguarded moment during a public lecture at Berkeley in 1975. 'The popularisation of the movement in non-spiritual terms was strictly for the purpose of gaining the attention of people who wouldn't have paid the movement much mind if it had been put in spiritual terms.'[6] In other words, the façade of science and therapy is no more than a 'come-on' for the real 'spiritual' Hindu message. (As Maharishi himself noted, 'If TM were a religion, it would be meaningful only to a small segment of the world.)'[7] And so in introductory lectures, recalls Vail Hamilton, 'we would more or less talk about the scientific effects upon the meditator and the relaxation and the benefits. After they'd signed up, we would go into discussing the cosmic consciousness; it was sort of like a surprise package.'[8]

After initiation, a great deal of pressure can be put upon the new meditator to get 'more involved', to go on weekend retreats, to advance to the stage of 'checker' by helping out at the local TM centre, then to become a teacher oneself, and even after that to undergo advanced courses, involving more and more occultist and oriental assumptions. Instruction is offered in *asana* (yoga posture exercises) and *pranayama* (breathing exercises), which like meditation are both stages of *raja yoga*, a discipline traditional in Hinduism for achieving union with God. Imperceptibly, the novice is led on from faith in a definable (if dangerous) experience, to faith in the movement's particular interpretation of that

[5] *The Holy Tradition* (no date or provenance).

[6] Quoted in Alexander, p. 2.

[7] Quoted in *The Fairfield Ledger*, 3 October 1975.

[8] *Penetrating*, p. 11.

experience – which is a very different thing. (*Cf.* Appendix 4.) Something happens when people meditate, of that there can be no doubt; but it is questionable, to say the least, whether that effect is the result of contacting an 'infinite field of Creative Intellect', and any further progress in TM based on that assumption is made purely as a step of faith.

R. D. Scott compares the teaching of TM to a drug habit. 'TM provides the mainstay of the teacher's life, world view and in many cases, his livelihood . . . In order to get higher, it is necessary to turn more and more people on to the experience. When an initiator has taught the technique to a specified number of novices, he is eligible for a "rest-and-rounding" course free of charge. In this way a teacher supports his "enlightenment habit". When he is not "rushing on to enlightenment" at a rest-and-rounding course, he is energetically pushing TM.'[9]

In February 1976 the New Jersey District Court was asked to decide whether or not TM was a religious practice. A group of concerned citizens filed a case against Maharishi, claiming that the teaching of TM in the state's public schools violated the US Constitution, which forbids instruction in religion. Late in 1977, the Court issued its opinion; it had no doubts; 'no inference was possible except that the teaching of SCI/TM and the *puja* are religious in nature'.[10]

The reasons for Judge Meanor's certainty will become clear if we examine the real facts about the *puja* and *mantra.*

(a) The puja

You are ushered into a room containing two chairs and an altar. The altar is a table covered with a white sheet, on which are a candle, an incense holder, and between them a picture of Guru Dev. In front lie a brass plate, three small dishes, and a piece of camphor in a brass holder. The three dishes contain rice, water, and a brown powder.

[9] Scott, pp. 134–135.
[10] *TM in Court* (the complete text of the Federal Court's opinion) (Berkeley, California, 1978), p. 72.

After promising never to reveal the details of your experience, you stand by your initiator before the altar, and watch as he dips a flower into the water and sprinkles the brass plate. He starts muttering in Sanskrit.

He places the items you have brought (handkerchief, fruit and flowers) on the brass plate together with water, rice and brown powder. The muttering develops into a chant, then breaks into song. After lighting an incense stick at the candle, the teacher uses it to light the camphor, which he then waves about before the picture, tracing circles in the air. Finally, as he places the last few flowers on the plate, the singing comes to an end, and with a carefully rehearsed, sweeping gesture he indicates that you should kneel with him before the altar. (Because of the stage-management, not many people refuse.)

As you both kneel, he begins to whisper one word over and over again. This is your *mantra*. Gradually the sound becomes clearer and louder, and then, with motions and nods, he invites you to join in. After a few minutes of chanting in concert, you are allowed to resume your seat, where you learn to chant more and more quietly, until eventually you are simply thinking the sound. You have been initiated.

What exactly have you just experienced? 'A mere gesture of ceremonial thanksgiving,' says the movement. 'A simple expression of gratitude to the long line of teachers who have passed on the technique down through the centuries.' But if this is so, it seems hard to explain why Jerry Jarvis (President of the TM movement in the United States) should insist, 'Initiation without the *puja* is like a Cadillac without gas.'[11] It is the *puja*, in other words, which supplies the power behind TM.

Should you ask your initiator for an English translation of his Sanskrit chant, you will be refused. Only qualified teachers are allowed to read the meaning of the *puja*. Why should this be, you might think, if the *puja* is merely an innocuous song of thanksgiving?

[11] Scott, p. 55.

The answer – as the New Jersey Court realised – is that the *puja* is actually much more. 'No words of gratitude or thanks appear in the English translation of the *puja* chant. The chant clearly is labelled "Invocation" twice. An invocation is the invoking or calling upon a spirit, a principle, a person or a deity for aid . . . The chant clearly invokes the spirit or deity of Guru Dev . . . '[12]

Thus every single person initiated into TM is deliberately, and misleadingly, implicated in a ceremony of worship to Hindu gods. To demonstrate just how blatant this is, I have included the English translation of the *puja* as Appendix I; I think even a cursory glance will show quite readily why the movement is not keen for the novice to see it. The *puja* hymn is made up of three elements, none of which would be the willing expression of most non-Hindu initiates:

Part 1: a recitation of the names of those who have passed on the knowledge. The list includes historical figures, semi-legendary ones, and mythological divine persons too. Each person mentioned is attributed divine status.
Part 2: seventeen offerings to Guru Dev, each stating 'I bow down' to him.
Part 3: a hymn of praise and adoration to Guru Dev, hailing him as God incarnate.

The movement replies that the naming of gods in the *puja* is just a matter of traditional form, and points out that the Hippocratic Oath (sworn by all doctors) incorporates the names of Greek deities. But this is just misleading. For one thing, the Greek gods no longer represent a living religious tradition: nobody believes in them any more. However, the gods of the *puja* are identified with a major religion which is still alive and well. And, more important, the references to gods in the Hippocratic Oath are passing, unimportant prefatory matter: indeed, the *Encyclopaedia Britannica* misses

[12] *TM in Court*, p. 41.

them out altogether when quoting the Oath. But try to take the names of gods out of the *puja*, and all you have left is a meaningless string of conjunctions, prepositions and adjectives.

Why, then, the deception? What does Maharishi think he stands to gain by putting unbelievers through an incomprehensible Hindu service? For our answer, we must look at the *mantra* which is the outcome of the *puja* ceremony.

(b) The mantra

There is nothing magical about the *mantra*, insists Anthony Campbell. 'The *mantra* could be thought of as a template, or seed crystal, which gives a pattern to the psychophysical structure. It is an organizing element; it supplies a pattern.'[13] The important thing is not its meaning, but the vibrational qualities which it possesses. The vibrations cause specific mental effects, and this is why teachers must be trained carefully in order to enable them skilfully to pick the correct *mantra* for any person they have to initiate.

In their American bestseller *TM*, three meditators, Bloomfield, Cain and Jaffe, claim that the technique for *mantra* selection is an 'ancient tradition', a 'systematic procedure' going back at least 6,970 years. The movement has hinted that personality, occupation, physical type, religious background and position in life all need to be taken into account in selecting the appropriate *mantra*.

Maharishi himself writes, 'But one thing is important to know, and that is that there are thousands of *mantras* and all have their specific values, specific qualities and are suitable for specific types of people . . . if the qualities of the energy impulses created by the sound of the *mantra* rightly correspond to the energy impulses of the man, only then will it be of real value. Any wrong choice of the *mantra* is sure to create unbalance in the harmony of the man's life.'[14]

In fact, this is totally false. There are only sixteen mantras

[13] Campbell, *op. cit.*, p. 26.
[14] *Meditations*, pp. 185–186.

34

in use. The sole criterion used for selecting the right one is the new meditator's age group!

The 'ancient tradition' goes all the way back to 1973 precisely, when Maharishi changed around his previous *mantra* list.

Does the meaning matter? If not, one wonders why so much secrecy is observed. Not even teachers are told the precise meanings of their *mantras*. Once, however, in a teacher training course at La Antilla in Spain, Maharishi gave a hint when he was asked directly, 'Are the gods we bow down to in the *puja* the same as the *mantras*?' In front of several hundred witnesses, he answered, 'Yes.'[15]

There appears to be abundant evidence that the *mantras* are all connected with the names of gods, and continue the invocation of them which is begun in the *puja*. Richard Scott, for example, eventually received the *mantra Shri aiing namah*, which, he realized with a shock, meant 'Oh most beautiful AIING, I bow down to you.' Since he had read the *Tantra Asana*, and knew that Aiing was the name of a Hindu creator god, this experience started many questions in his mind about the probity of the movement.

But does it matter? Perhaps, indeed, the Maharishi does derive a secret thrill from knowing that he has fooled the Western world into chanting the names of Eastern gods for forty minutes a day: but what difference does it make? 'After all,' most folk will say, 'it's the intention that counts. If someone tricks me into chanting something I don't really mean, I'm not really worshipping, am I?'

But a Hindu guru would answer, 'Yes, you are.' Worship in Hinduism is not seen as a matter of the thoughts and intents of the heart, as in Christianity; instead it is a matter of the vibrations which your chanting creates in the atmosphere around you. By chanting the *mantra*, you are arousing the interest and patronage of the particular god whose name you are citing. The *mantra* works its supernatural effect independently of any faith you may possess.

[15] Scott, p. 93.

Thus, whether or not he believes in the reality of the gods or demons whose influence lies behind the *mantras*, the meditator is being introduced to a religious practice which is never fully explained to him, and which he would most probably eschew if it were. The *puja* is the way in to supernatural involvement; it provides the first link with the shadowy spiritual powers whose help is being sought, and draws down their attention upon the new meditator. He then unwittingly extends their influence in his life by innocently chanting their names in his *mantra*. The whole automatic process can fairly be described as a confidence trick, of truly cosmic proportions.

A 'scientifically verifiable technique' – or exposure to unnamed dangers? As we shall see, the evidence suggests that some kind of supernatural peril is most definitely involved.

7
Dangerous side-effects

13 October, 1977, was a big day for the ungrateful human race. Little though most of us realized it, that was the historic date upon which Maharishi Mahesh Yogi finally declared all nations 'invincible'. In other words, there is no need for us to worry about war any more.

Because of the increased numbers of meditators worldwide, nations which until now have been at loggerheads can stop fearing each other; the vibrations set up by the meditators have cancelled out all hostile threats. 'World consciousness' has been raised as the total number of meditators in the world approaches the magic figure of 1%.

President Sadat's visit to Jerusalem in November is cited as the first evidence of the transformation of consciousness. The Age of Enlightenment is almost upon us! ('Never mind the total collapse of the Mid-East peace initiative,' commented Mark Albrecht tartly, 'and the armed Israeli invasion of Lebanon.')[1] And this 'Maharishi Effect' upon the total world population can be noticed on a local level too: a town with a high percentage of meditators, says the movement, will see a drop in crime and aggressive thinking. There is even a claim that tornadoes have been seen to turn away from towns with a high proportion of meditators.

By the 'EME', or 'Extended Maharishi Effect', meditation is supposed to have an impact upon neighbouring places too. Thus San Bernardino, in California, is being claimed as a place which has been cleaned up by the amount of meditation going on in nearby Los Angeles. Thinking big, Maharishi has moved teams of teachers to Japan, Korea, the Philippines, Nepal, and other countries near China, in order to bombard Red China – 'the greatest danger to peace and harmony in the world'[2] – with helpful vibrations.

In fact, however, even if there were a relationship between a drop in the crime rate of a town and an increase in TM initiations – which is certainly unproven – it would not enhance Maharishi's credibility one iota.

The crime rate, first of all, depends on all sorts of other factors: the make-up of the population; juvenile trends; which precise laws are on the statute book; and thus it is not an easy job to determine exactly how much any one factor has contributed to a decline. More crucially, though, no research is done by anyone into how many people have paid their fee, been initiated, and then simply stopped meditating. Richard Scott, an ex-teacher of meditation himself, estimates that the drop-out rate may be as high as 50% in some places. If this is the case, it means that no – one (least of all the Maharishi) has the wildest idea of exactly how much meditation is actually going on.

But at least the 'Maharishi Effect' illustrates very graphically the movement's belief in the power of unseen spiritual vibrations. When someone meditates, he is not

[1] *SCP Newsletter*, vol. 4, no. 3 (April 1978), p. 1.
[2] *Ibid.*, p. 1.

simply tapping a source of power within himself; he is affecting an intangible, mysterious force outside of his body. The explanatory booklet *The Holy Tradition*, given to trainee teachers, makes this quite clear. Speaking of the *puja*, it declares, 'The entire purpose of the ceremony we are going to describe is to tune ourselves to the source of energy and wisdom from which Transcendental Meditation stems.'[3] And Maharishi has admitted quite openly that the purpose of chanting the *mantra* is 'to produce an effect in some other world, to draw the attention of those higher beings or gods living there. The entire knowledge of the mantras . . . is devoted to man's connection, to man's communication with the higher beings in a different strata (*sic*) of creation'.[4]

This is why on a teacher's training course 'a couple of pundits [Vedic scholars] were flown in from India, and for a couple of evenings we listened to them chant from the Vedas. The meaning of their chants was not explained, but it was supposed to produce a very spiritual atmosphere that would be conducive to our "evolution".'[5] It is also why, during the New Jersey trial, Maharishi sent three of his most trusted and powerful 'governors' to live in Newark, where the Federal Court was situated, to beam the vibrations of their psycho-spiritual power towards the judge. TM believes firmly in the existence of an occult realm which can be contacted at will (or even unwittingly!) and can confer magic powers upon humanity.

Since 1977, the occult trappings of TM have become increasingly explicit. It began with a report given by three teachers at Fairmont Hotel, San Francisco, that research at Maharishi European Research University had achieved a 'new breakthrough in the development of human potential'. The three claimed to be able to levitate their bodies and move through the air without any material support.[6]

[3] *The Holy Tradition.*

[4] *Meditations*, pp. 17–18.

[5] Scott, p. 37.

[6] *San Francisco Chronicle*, 3 May 1977, p. 13.

Since then such powers have gone on offer to the general public as well. Some TM advertisements are currently reading:

LEARN NEW TECHNIQUES
UNFOLD THE MARVELS OF YOUR
CONSCIOUSNESS
LEVITATION – FLYING – INVISIBILITY
STRENGTH OF AN ELEPHANT
MASTERY OVER NATURE
STUDENTS INVITED TO DEVELOP POWERS OF A
SUPERMAN

Transcendental Meditation is dabbling in a murky realm in which there can be evil, destructive forces and, unlike many forms of mysticism, it takes no precautions. William Johnston, an expert on mystical theology, has pointed out that 'all religions know of a mysticism of evil', and that because of the dangers of a possible bad 'trip' while meditating, traditional mysticism requires the meditator to have 'undergone a conversion and be totally dedicated to good'.[7] There is no such requirement in TM enrolment. What we know about possession and demonology seems to suggest that it may be possible for a human being to bring himself to the attention of spirit beings of an evil kind who would normally pay no attention to him, and against whose devices he is absolutely powerless. Is TM a gateway to possession?

Teachers returning from training courses have felt the presence of intangible, unseen 'guardian angels' with them. But the 'angels' can turn nasty upon occasion. Five months after Susan Scott began to practise TM, she had visions of demonic, ghoulish creatures as well as creatures of light

[7] William Johnston, *Silent Music: The Science of Meditation* (New York, 1974), p. 95. See also G. R. Lewis's discussion in his *What Everyone should Know about Transcendental Meditation* (Glendale, California, 1975), pp. 70–72.

39

floating past her through walls and doors. Apparently, she found, this was not an unusual experience for a meditator, and Charles Lutes (Director of TM in the USA) counselled her that the ghoulish creatures were demons. She must never on any account stare into their eyes.

Vail Hamilton, another meditator, remembers that 'as my consciousness expanded I began to become aware of the presence of spirit-beings sitting on either side of me when I was meditating and sometimes they would sit on my bed.'[8] She also found herself involved in the beginnings of clairvoyance, telepathy and astral travel. Other meditators have seen large pairs of green eyes floating around the room, have been thrown bodily across their bedrooms, and have experienced involuntary twitchings, jerkings and repetitive movements of the head. Whether or not one believes in any sort of supernatural, these symptoms cannot be indicative of a completely healthy state of affairs.

Maharishi has, of course, an answer for it – 'unstressing'. He compares the human mind to a box containing tightly packed balls of crushed cellophane. When the lid is taken off, all of the balls start trying to loosen themselves immediately, and this can radically change the arrangement of the box's contents. Experiencing relaxation through TM is like releasing the lid on the box. The mind's accumulated stresses – the balls of cellophane – start untangling themselves, and the sudden release can require too much reorientation for the meditator's mind to handle with comfort.

This is a view of the operation of stress which is completely unsupported by medical science. But whatever the real reason for it, 'unstressing' is a well-known phenomenon among advanced meditators; which makes it worrying that no novice is ever told about it. Greg Randolph, who taught meditation for five years, explains the dangers.

'When you're unstressing for a long time, large amounts of this stress can come out and actually condition angry

[8] *The Catholic Voice* 29 (17 November 1975).

40

moods and cause heart attacks and all kinds of different experiences, violent angry rages and all kinds of different unstress things . . .

A friend of mine who was reaching cosmic consciousness . . . was doing just a little extra meditation one day and he had a seizure of some kind and found he didn't have control over his body for a whole evening. He explained this as the stress leaving in great quantities as one approaches a higher state of consciousness . . .

There is also such a thing as the black-out phenomenon, where a person will black out and wake up three hours later and not know what happened. The Maharishi explains the black-out as a great release of stress to such a degree that it fogs your mind, and instantly you go to sleep . . . Nobody really knows for sure what is happening.[9]

But the dangers of Transcendental Meditation are highlighted most dramatically in the exceptionally high suicide rate among TM teachers. Kathy Filler remembers Charles Lutes admitting this to trainee teachers, and failing to provide any satisfactory reason for it. 'People were asking about the suicide rate – teachers were asking why so many were killing themselves. He said, "Well, in future incarnations, Maharishi will appear to them himself or Guru Dev, and give them their extra *mantra* . . . " '[10]

Responsible world religions have always treated the supernatural world with care, realism and objectivity. We are fighting not against flesh and blood, says the New Testament, but against powers of spiritual wickedness and darkness in heavenly realms.[11] TM's uncritical acceptance of anything the unseen world can provide prompts the question: does Maharishi know what he is doing? Or is the blind leading the blind into a supernatural man-trap?

[9] *Right On*, November 1975, p. 10.
[10] *Penetrating*, p. 10.
[11] Ephesians 6:12.

8
Fake objectivity

All over the world, says Maharishi, religion is dying. The 'inner light' of the great world faiths has disappeared. 'Only the rituals and dogma are found: the spirit has departed. That is why the followers of religion do not find fulfilment.'[1] But priest and parson, shaman and guru, all can now heave a sigh of relief: Maharishi has arrived to put things right!

He can do this, he says, because TM is really what the great religions are all about. 'Here in a simple practice is the fulfilment of every religion . . . it existed in the early days of every faith and has since been lost.'[2] No longer, for instance, need Christians puzzle over such cryptic statements as 'the kingdom of heaven is within you' or 'whoever has seen me, has seen the Father'. Jesus was referring to his meditation technique!

Furthermore, says *The Holy Tradition*, if in the future new religions spring up, that is what they will be about too. The central 'eternal truth' of all religions is exactly the same thing: a mental release system currently known as TM.

Anyone who has studied the origins of the great world religions, or indeed has spent a cursory five minutes with *The Varieties of Religious Experience*, will wonder at the glib assurance of these statements. In order to unite the diverse aims and activities in human cultural history which are subsumed under the label 'Religion', Transcendental Meditation would have to be a wonder of theological tightrope-walking and philosophical diplomacy. As things are, we can quite easily prove that it is no such thing.

[1] *SBAL*, p. 256.
[2] *SBAL*, p. 259.

Comparison of TM teaching with one great religion – Christianity – will reveal very quickly how many miles apart are the ideas of Jesus Christ and those of Maharishi Mahesh Yogi.

(a) What God is like

For Jesus Christ, God was unmistakably a *person*. He created the universe from nothing, and is not to be confused with it. He is not the same God who is worshipped in a variety of guises by different religions, but carefully guards his distinctiveness. This had always been the Jewish concept of God.

> I am the LORD, and there is no other,
>> besides me there is no God; ...
>
> I made the earth,
>> and created man upon it;
>
> it was my hands that stretched out the heavens,
>> and I commanded all their host ...
>
>> And there is no other god besides me,
>
> a righteous God and a Saviour;
>> there is none besides me.[3]

Maharishi's God, by contrast, is just 'It' – an impersonal quality, 'the essential Being in everyone'.[4] Far from being distinct from creation, and supreme over it, 'everywhere and in all circumstances Being, the essential constituent of creation, permeates everything. It is the omnipresent God for those who know and understand It, feel It and live It in their lives.'[5]

I need hardly say that this is an unabashedly Hindu viewpoint on God. The Bible teaches that man has been cut off from contact with the Creator God by his own acts of sinfulness, but according to TM, if we feel out of touch with

---

[3] Isaiah 45:5, 12, 21.
[4] *SBAL*, p. 283n.
[5] *SBAL*, p. 29.

God, the trouble is simply that we have not yet started to meditate. There is no impassable gulf yawning between the sinful human and the perfect God, for God is no more than the most highly developed part of creation, 'on the highest level of evolution'.[6]

When someone becomes a Christian, promised Jesus, 'My Father will love him and we will come to him and make our home with him.'[7] According to Maharishi, God the Father is there inside us already! God is just 'the essential Being in everyone. It forms the basis of every life; it is nothing other than one's own Self or Being.'[8]

A God who is a person – and a God who is a 'thing'. A Creator distinct from the work He has made – and a fully evolved constituent of ultimate reality. A holy individual with whom personal friendship is possible – and an intangible essence at the depths of one's being. There could hardly be more differences between Maharishi's God and Christ's!

(b) The meaning of life
The Bible always visualizes history as a straight line with a beginning and an end. What was, is past: what is future, has not yet been. By contrast, a Hindu sees time as an endless circle. What was, will be again; the future will be a repetition of the past. The universe is not groaning with the pain of birth-pangs, as the apostle Paul[9] put it, waiting for the ultimate resolution of history in the coming again of Jesus Christ, but is a never-ending cycle of births, deaths and rebirths.

Maharishi, of course, subscribes to the Hindu view. 'Generation after generation man is born anew. Each generation gives rise to new aspirations in life, new standards of thought

---

[6] *SBAL*, p. 277.
[7] John 14:23.
[8] *SBAL*, p. 283n.
[9] Romans 8:22.

and action, and brings a new quest for fulfilment.'[10] The universe is not heading for a great consummation, except of course for the 'Age of Enlightenment' which TM is destined to usher in. But even that will not be a final stopping-point.

A man's expectations about the future determine the way he lives. Someone with a great deal to look forward to will approach the business of living in a radically different way from a person with no hopes and ambitions. And when we see how much of the New Testament message is tied up with the second coming of Jesus; how much that one point in time is supposed to condition a Christian's awareness of his circumstances; we realize again that a massive difference exists between the TM philosophy and the Christian hope.

> Besides this you know what hour it is, how it is full time now for you to wake from sleep. For salvation is nearer to us now than when we first believed; the night is far gone, the day is at hand.[11]

> Since all these things are thus to be dissolved, what sort of persons ought you to be? . . . according to his promise we wait for new heavens and a new earth in which righteousness dwells.[12]

It is difficult to see how the people who believe these claims can align themselves with a man who proclaims, 'TM is the only way to salvation and success in life; there is no other way.'[13]

Because Christians believe that there is a meaning and a progression in time, Christianity has become associated with all sorts of relief movements and social improvements throughout the centuries. Because of his cyclic view of time – those who suffer in this life will be coming round again for another shot anyway – Maharishi displays a rather chill-

[10] *SBAL*, p. 305.
[11] Romans 13:11–12.
[12] 2 Peter 3:11,13.
[13] *BG*, p. 228.

ing lack of concern for the social problems of the world. Apart from expansive claims such as that wars would cease for generations if 10% of us meditated, or that TM can 'change a hard, cruel nature to one of tolerance and compassion',[14] Maharishi's basic attitude is one of complacent unconcern. Asked at a reception in New Delhi what TM would do for the poor of India, Maharishi answered, 'They will be hungry but they will be happy.'[15] And for all his drum-beating about drug abuse prevention, rehabilitation of criminals, and so on, he has started not one solitary scheme or project to advance social welfare. All of the money he receives (and why should he charge so much for explaining a technique which is supposed to be every man's birthright?) goes straight into the TM coffers. It hardly compares with the teaching of a certain Galilean carpenter.

(c) The truth about humanity

As we observed a moment ago, the Bible is hard-headed and unflattering about human pretensions. The world is flawed because man has rebelled against God. There is a barrier between God and man because of human selfishness and independence. Men cannot help themselves: God must take the initiative to rescue them from their plight.

Not so, says Maharishi. This problem of sin is a very insignificant thing. 'Man's life is meant to be a bridge between divine intelligence and the whole of creation ... Every man is capable of spreading divine splendour throughout creation ... Each man is capable of living a life of full values. If he fails to do this he brings shame on himself, and he abuses the glory of almighty God present within and around him.'[16]

No moral struggles. No conflicts. Through TM 'very easily a sinner comes out of the field of sin and becomes a virtuous man'.[17] Anthony Campbell puts the position succinctly:

[14] *SBAL*, p. 221.

[15] William Jefferson, *The Story of the Maharishi* (New York, 1975), p. 35.

[16] *SBAL*, p. 83.

[17] *Meditations*, p. 119.

46

'Other traditions have said: Become moral and then meditate. Maharishi says meditate and you will then become a moral person.'[18]

Thus TM claims to be able to bring about the 'speedy and effective' rehabilitation of delinquents and criminals (a claim the movement has not so far substantiated). There is really no freedom of choice: the meditator becomes morally perfect without any effort or thought, whether he wants to or not. In Cosmic Consciousness 'his thought, speech and action are guided naturally by the divine will'.[19]

The Bible, on the other hand, speaks of the Christian as a battleground: of an old, evil nature warring against the new; of the power of the Holy Spirit, but also of the ever-present reality of temptation. God may transform your nature, but he will not take away your freedom of choice. To be good involves a moral decision, often at some cost: not the painless application of a mental relaxation technique.

Maharishi's view of human nature lends a very sinister tone to his pronouncements about TM's future plans. Bad actions, he says, set up vibrations which affect the whole of society. (For instance, whenever a mother slaps her child in anger, 'then she has slapped or beaten the whole universe, and produced an atmosphere of crying and hatred, suffering and discord, not only in the child but in everything around and in the whole universe'.)[20] Thus anyone who is creating bad vibrations (in other words, who is not a meditator) is a menace to society. And so, incredibly, the TM movement looks forward to a day when TM will be law, and non-meditators will be *forced* to learn the technique.

I heard this statement very clearly, and I'll never forget it. Jerry [Jarvis, US president of the TM movement] told us that . . . since it is illegal for anyone to throw their garbage

[18] Quoted in Kroll, p. 165.
[19] *SBAL*, p. 99.
[20] *SBAL*, p. 228.

out into the street because it inconveniences other people, it should also be illegal for individuals to throw their tensions out into society, and therefore everyone should be forced, there should be a law – these were Jarvis's exact words – there should be a law that everyone should have to practise TM.[21]

Far-fetched, impossible? At the moment, perhaps; most people simply laughed when they heard that Maharishi had already picked his World Government, as far back as 1976. But the insidious spread of meditation devotees into high-ranking positions in government, the armed forces and medicine, suggests a menacing note in Maharishi's cryptic words:

> There has not been and there will not be a place for the unfit. The fit will lead, and if the unfit are not coming along there is no place for them ... In the Age of Enlightenment there is no place for ignorant people. The ignorant will be made enlightened by a few orderly, enlightened people moving around ... Non-existence of the unfit has been the law of nature.[22]

(b) Right and wrong
It will be seen from the foregoing that TM is not very interested in the problem of personal moral weakness. 'You get an idea of renunciation during meditation,' said Campbell, in answer to a question on the subject, 'but it is renouncing of peripheral things, such as thinking about your failings and your wanting to be better.'[23] Buoyed up by the assurance that no real change of lifestyle or habits is necessary to make him into a moral person, a meditator can (ironically enough) become more self-centred and egotistical than before. This

[21] Alexander, p. 3.

[22] Maharishi Mahesh Yogi, *Inauguration of the Dawn of the Age of Enlightenment* (Fairfield, Iowa, 1975), p. 47.

[23] Quoted in Kroll, p. 168.

was Vail Hamilton's experience. 'As I began meditating more and more, I noticed a growing pride and insensitivity to others in myself – even though I felt more calm and confident than ever before. I realized I was becoming, in fact, my own god.'[24]

The further one advances in TM, the less traditional standards of right and wrong matter. For a person in 'CC', 'the question of a suitable criterion by which to judge right and wrong does not arise'.[25] The ultimate aim of meditation is to reach 'a state of consciousness which will justify any action'.[26]

There are no absolute standards. 'Certainly right and wrong are relative terms, and, therefore, nothing in relative existence can be said to be absolutely right or absolutely wrong. But even so, right and wrong can only be judged by their influence for good and bad. If something produces a good influence everywhere it can be said to be right.'[27]

In order to produce a 'good influence', then, a meditator could theoretically justify murder, robbery, lies and rape. What does Maharishi define as 'good'? 'That which helps the process of evolution,' is his answer. And since 'evolution' is identical with the progress of the TM movement, remarks Brooks Alexander, 'the practical impact of this dictum is to make the moral value of all behaviour relative to the effect it has on the fortunes of the TM movement'![28]

What does Jesus Christ have to say about personal failure? It is at this point that we encounter the very heart of the Christian 'good news'. The Bible teaches that Christ (the unique Son of God, not merely one spiritual master among many in the Maharishi's Holy Tradition) became a human being in order to die and, by dying, cancel out the penalty of human sins. And since for our sake he made him to be sin

[24] Quoted in Means, p. 139.
[25] *SBAL*, p. 225.
[26] *BG*, p. 76.
[27] *SBAL*, p. 224.
[28] Alexander, p. 3.

4

who knew no sin, so that in him we might become the righteousness of God,[29] he is now able to inhabit a human life, bringing power to conquer temptation and discover God's reality. 'And,' added his earliest followers, 'there is no other name under heaven, given among men, by which we must be saved.'[30]

This idea comes into direct, inescapable conflict with Maharishi's sweeping claim that TM is 'the only way out of the field of sin',[31] a method 'without which there is *no way out*'.[32] Through incredible, unimaginable suffering ('I don't think Christ ever suffered,' remarked Maharishi),[33] Christ made a way back to God which no human effort could ever have achieved. He did something immeasurably greater for the human race than teaching it a technique of mind relaxation. Neither did he charge a week's wages in order to explain it.

9
Epilogue

Once there was a village of farmers, living in poverty on the east bank of a river, across which they could dimly see waving fields of corn on the farther shore. Their sorrow was great, because they knew that the river was too treacherous to cross. They had boats, but did not venture out too far into the current for fear of being swept away.

One day, a giggling guru from the Himalayas arrived and convinced the chief men of the village that the river could be crossed. 'All the power that you need', he said, 'is

[29] 2 Corinthians 5:21.
[30] Acts 4:12.
[31] *BG*, p. 203.
[32] *BG*, p. 299.
[33] *Meditations*, p. 123.

within yourselves. You need only stop doubting and launch out your boats.' So, unaware of the dangers they were going to encounter, several of the young men took to the water. None reached the opposite bank, and some were swept away and drowned.

However, since dead men tell no tales, and since the guru spoke with an air of authority, many of the people came to believe that their dead friends *had* in fact reached the other side, and began to launch out after them. At that point another stranger arrived in the village.

He wore the clothes of a humble journeyman carpenter, but spoke with the same assurance of tone as the guru. 'You cannot do it,' he warned the people. 'No boat you make will be strong enough to take you over. What you need is a bridge.'

'And who can build it?' they scornfully replied. 'No one could construct a bridge of such a length. We will continue to use our boats. Many of our friends are already across.'

'I tell you the truth,' said the carpenter sorrowfully, 'no man of you will ever arrive on the other shore without my help.'

At this the people were so enraged that they took up stones and clubbed him to death. Then they left his body lying on the dusty path and returned to their boat-building.

But three days later the body disappeared. No – one could tell where it had gone. And another marvel had taken place, for spanning the river, from shore to shore, linking the village of poverty to the shores of plenty, there stood a wonderful, new bridge.

It stands still for all who will walk across.

Appendix 1
The Puja ceremony

INVOCATION OF THE HOLY TRADITION

Whether pure or impure, or whether full of purities or impurities,

Whosoever remembers the lotus-eyed Lord gains inner and outer purity.

INVOCATION

To Lord Narayan, to lotus-born Brahma the Creator, to Vaishistha, to Shakti and his son Parashar,

To Vyasa, to Shukadeva, to the great Gaudapada, to Govinda, ruler among the yogis, to his disciple

Shri Shankaracharya, to his disciples Padma-Padam, Hasta-Malakam,

To him, Trotakacharya, to Vartik-kar, to others, to the Tradition of our Masters, I bow down.

To the abode of the wisdom of the Shrutis, Smritis and Puranas, to the abode of kindness, to the feet of the Lord Shankaracharya, to the emancipator of the world, I bow down.

To Shankaracharya the emancipator, hailed as Krishna and Badarayana, to the commentator of the Brahma Sutras, I bow down, to the Lord I bow down again and again.

At whose door the whole galaxy of gods pray for perfection day and night,

Adorned by immeasurable glory, preceptor of the whole world, having bowed down to Him, we gain fulfilment.

Skilled in dispelling the cloud of ignorance of the people,

the gentle emancipator, Brahmananda Saraswati, the supreme teacher, full of brilliance, on Him we meditate.

Offering invocation to the lotus feet of Shri Guru Dev, I bow down.

Offering a seat to the lotus feet of Shri Guru Dev, I bow down.

Offering a bath to the lotus feet of Shri Guru Dev, I bow down.

Offering a cloth to the lotus feet of Shri Guru Dev, I bow down.

Offering sandal paste to the lotus feet of Shri Guru Dev, I bow down.

Offering full unbroken rice to the lotus feet of Shri Guru Dev, I bow down.

Offering a flower to the lotus feet of Shri Guru Dev, I bow down.

Offering incense to the lotus feet of Shri Guru Dev, I bow down.

Offering light to the lotus feet of Shri Guru Dev, I bow down.

Offering water to the lotus feet of Shri Guru Dev, I bow down.

Offering fruit to the lotus feet of Shri Guru Dev, I bow down.

Offering water to the lotus feet of Shri Guru Dev, I bow down.

Offering betel leaf to the lotus feet of Shri Guru Dev, I bow down.

Offering coconut to the lotus feet of Shri Guru Dev, I bow down.

Offering camphor flame

White as camphor, the incarnation of kindness, the essence of creation, garlanded by the Serpent King,

Ever dwelling in the lotus of my heart, Lord Shiva with Mother Divine, to Him I bow down.

Offering light to the lotus feet of Shri Guru Dev, I bow down.

Offering water to the lotus feet of Shri Guru Dev, I bow down.

Offering a handful of flowers

Guru in the glory of Brahma, Guru in the glory of Vishnu, Guru in the glory of the great Lord Shiva, Guru in the supreme Transcendent personified; therefore to Shri Guru Dev, adorned by glory, I bow down.

The Unbounded as the endless canopy of the sky, the Omnipresent in all creation, the sign of That has been revealed by Him who was That; therefore to Him, to Shri Guru Dev, I bow down.

Guru Dev, Shri Brahmananda, in the glory of the bliss of the Absolute, in the glory of transcendental joy, in the glory of Unity, the very embodiment of knowledge, who is beyond the universe like the sky, as the goal of 'That thou art' and other (Shrutis which grant eternal Unity of life.)

The One, the Eternal, the Pure, the Immoveable, the Witness of all intellects, whose status transcends thought, the Transcendent along with the three gunas, the true preceptor, to Shri Guru Dev I bow down.

The blinding darkness of ignorance has been removed by the application of the ointment of knowledge, the eye of knowledge has been opened by Him; therefore to Him, to Shri Guru Dev, I bow down.

Offering a handful of flowers to the lotus feet of Shri Guru Dev, I bow down.

(This is the translation which appears in the movement's own handbook *The Holy Tradition*.)

Appendix 2
The TM Mantra List

(a) As in use in 1970:

Age in years	Male	Female
5–10	Ing	Im
10–16	Ing	Im
16–30	Aaing	Aaim

Between the ages of 5 and 10, a special 'walking technique' or 'children's technique' is used for saying the *mantra*.

(b) As revised in 1973. A fuller list, but hardly 'thousands'; and why the disappearance of the male/female distinction?

Age	Mantra
10–12	Eng
12–14	Em
14–16	Enga
16–18	Ema
18–20	Aeng
20–22	Aem
22–24	Aenga
24–26	Aema
26–30	Shiring

Age	Mantra
30–35	Shirim
35–40	Hiring
40–45	Hirim
45–50	Kiring
50–55	Kirim
55–60	Shyam
60–65 and older	Shyama

NB. As other ex-meditators have supplied lists differing in some crucial details from this (see, *e.g.,* Greg Randolph's list in Means), it is likely that further revisions have been made to the 'ancient' tradition.

Appendix 3
Advice to Christians

Whenever I give a talk on Transcendental Meditation, two questions are sure to come up in the question time afterwards. The first is 'But don't Christians meditate? Isn't it referred to in the Bible? What's the difference between the way Maharishi does it, and Christian meditation?'

This is a good question. And in answering it I intend to say nothing about the mediaeval mystics already referred to, about whose spiritual achievements I am personally rather dubious. Those who wish to can investigate their claims for themselves. Here I shall confine myself to what the Bible itself has to say about meditation.

It is certainly true that the Old Testament (and interestingly, never the New, in this sense) mentions 'meditation' a few times. Four Hebrew words are used in all, and in every case the type of 'meditation' envisaged involves *use of the conscious mind.* Biblical meditation means the generation of active thoughts in one of three areas (meditation about God's person, works, or statements) and *never* the suppression of constructive thought in order to chant with a blank mind. An example of each word will demonstrate this clearly.

'I will meditate *on all thy work*', Psalm 77:12.
'I will meditate *on thy precepts*', Psalm 119: 15.
'How I love *thy law*! It is my meditation', Psalm 119: 97.
'The lips and thoughts of my assailants are *against me* all the day long', Lamentations 3: 62.

Christian meditation, then, means consciously deliberating upon some facet of God's revelation, and allowing it slowly to take a grip of one's mind and thought until one becomes 'transformed by the renewal *of your mind*' (Rom. 12: 2). The transformation worked by Christian meditation is not of a psychic, mystical kind, but involves conscious thought and deliberation.

Considering that Jesus said 'do not heap up empty phrases as the Gentiles do' (Mt. 6: 7); considering that he defined true worship as 'in spirit and *truth*'; considering that the apostle Paul said he would rather pray with the understanding than without (1 Cor. 14: 14–19); it should be obvious that techniques of mindless meditation find no sanction in the New Testament, and much to discourage their use. Jesus taught his disciples to pray in words, to converse with God, not to sit around mumbling the names of Asiatic divinities.

The second question usually asked by Christians is 'How can I best talk to people involved in TM?' There are three reasons why this is difficult. First, the meditator has an in-built sense of superiority; he has the key to all religions, including yours, while you have not even had the basic experience which lies behind religious theory. Thus you can expect an attitude of 'There's nothing *you* can teach *me*'. Second, his reliance is upon direct, subjective experience – not reason – and his thinking may be very confused. Do not expect logical arguments and do not become frustrated if his comments seem random and uncomprehending.

Third, Maharishi has warned meditators against showing too much interest in the religious views of other people. 'A man leading a life according to the spiritual code of his own religion will find the truth of life without confusing himself by a comparative study of different religions,' he warns (*SBAL* 225). And so the meditator will generally project a cold lack of interest: 'Why should I confuse myself by studying your religious views? I have my own.'

There are certain arguments, however, which can be effective. Here are a few.

(1) You can argue from the deceptions within the TM movement. Does he know what the *puja* means? Or how *mantras* are selected? Or about 'unstressing' and the suicide problem? You must be able to show him that even marginal involvement of the 'forty minutes a day' type has its dangers.

(2) You can show the clear differences between religions. Maharishi's slick statement that all religions centre on the same 'eternal truth' is clearly untrue, and you can show why with just a little knowledge. (If the root of Christianity and Islam is the same, for example, why did Mohammed bother to found a new religion? Why did the Buddha feel so dissatisfied with the Hindu tradition?)

(3) You can talk about the fact of personal failure (which TM glibly ignores). Meditators have consciences, and cannot always blind themselves to the fact that TM is failing to make as sizeable a moral impact upon their lives as they would wish.

(4) You can open his eyes to what real Christianity is. Maharishi paints a picture of a religion subsisting uneasily upon a diet of moral exhortations and scare stories about hell fire (*SBAL* 257–8). Most meditators have no intelligent idea of the genuine Christian claim.

(5) You can explore the unanswered questions which TM skates around. Is all stress *ipso facto* a bad thing? Would famous writers and artists have produced their greatest work

without stress in their lives, pain and pressure? If TM is simply a functional technique, what is it *for*? Una Kroll points out, 'If there is a technique, there is the question of what it is to be used for; there is a responsibility on people who set something like this going to think about how it is to be used socially' (Kroll, p. 165.) And how does the meditator know that his interpretation (or rather Maharishi's interpretation!) of his totally subjective experience is the correct one? Could he not be involved, whatever the seeming benefits, in a form of 'spiritual masturbation', a 'psychic leucotomy'? (These phrases are borrowed from Roy Clements' *God and the Gurus*, IVP, which I strongly commend for its critique of mysticism in general.)

Remember, however, to do all this in a spirit of love, gentleness and understanding. Victims of confidence tricks are not always grateful to those who point out their mistake! And remember that ultimately the battle is a spiritual one, not against flesh and blood but against the hosts of wickedness in spiritual realms (Eph. 6: 12) whom the meditator is unconsciously invoking. And that means that you need the 'whole armour of God'.

Appendix 4
Other possible interpretations of the kind of religious experience provided by TM

'Now from my own unforgettable experience I know well that there is a state in which the bonds of the personal nature of life seem to have fallen away from us and we experience an undivided unity. But I do not know – what the soul willingly imagines and indeed is bound to imagine (mine too once did it) – that in this I had attained to a union with the primal being or the godhead . . . I can elicit from those experiences only that in them I reached an undifferentiable unity of myself without form or content . . . in the honest and sober account of the responsible understanding the unity is nothing but the unity of this soul of mine, whose "ground" I have reached . . . and not "the soul of the All"; a defined and particular being and not "Being" . . . ' Martin Buber, *Between Man and Man* (New York, 1965), p. 24.

'It is possible to "become Brahman" without for that reason entering into loving communion with God; and this is, in fact, what the monistic mystics do. Divested as they are of all their moral trappings they are content to rest in the quiet contemplation of their own souls; having reached the immortal they can conceive of nothing beyond. They are blinded by their own self-sufficiency, for having conquered desire they cannot rekindle desire itself and direct it to its proper goal which is God.' R. C. Zaehner, *Hindu and Muslim Mysticism* (New York, 1969), p. 15.

'The loss of personality while consciousness is retained during the illusion of union with the "All" leads to the belief that the nature of the "All" is impersonal consciousness. Actually the meditator is merely experiencing his own altered consciousness which has been temporarily depersonalized by the suppression of perceptions and intellect in meditation.' David Haddon, 'A Christian Orientation towards Eastern Mysticism', *Incite* I (1), p. 8.

Abbreviations

Alexander: Brooks Alexander, *Who is this man and what does he want?* (Berkeley, California, 1976).

BG: Maharishi Mahesh Yogi, *On the Bhagavad-Gita: A New Translation and Commentary* (Baltimore, 1967).

Kroll: Una Kroll, *TM: A Signpost for the World* (London, 1974).

Means: Pat Means, *The Mystical Maze* (San Bernardino, Ca., 1977; available from Campus Crusade, 105 London Road, Reading R91 5BY, UK).

Meditations: Maharishi Mahesh Yogi, *Meditations of Maharishi Mahesh Yogi* (New York, 1973).

Penetrating: TM: Penetrating the Veil of Deception, compilation of articles by Spiritual Counterfeits Project, Berkeley, California.

SBAL: Maharishi Mahesh Yogi, *The Science of Being and the Art of Living* (new revised edn., London, 1966).

Scott: R. D. Scott, *Transcendental Misconceptions* (San Diego, California, 1978).

For further reading

The rising of the Moon
John Allan
An examination of the Unification Church of Sun Myung
Moon – its history, teachings and methods of
recruitment.
64 pp.

God and the gurus
R. D. Clements
A look at the Divine Light Mission, Hare Krishna
and TM, contrasting eastern mysticism with
Christian truth.
64 pp.

Christian meditation
Edmund P. Clowney
The Bible often tells us to meditate. But what is
Christian meditation, and how does it differ
from eastern techniques?
48 pp.

Inter-Varsity Press, 38 De Montfort Street, Leicester LE1 7GP